DAVE'S BAD JOKES 2

Dave Moore is a radio presenter, podcast host and music producer. His Today FM morning show is the biggest commercial music radio show in Ireland. He is also passionate about sneakers, languages, guitars and DIY.

Dave lives in Portmarnock with his wife, the artist and illustrator Tracy Sheridan, and their four children.

DAVE'S BAD JOKES 2

DAVE MOORE

GILL BOOKS

Gill Books
Hume Avenue
Park West
Dublin 12

www.gillbooks.ie

Gill Books is an imprint of M.H. Gill and Co.

© Dave Moore 2025

9781804584262

Design and layout by Liz White Designs

Edited by Jane Rogers

Proofread by Susan McKeever

Printed and bound by Scandbook, Sweden

This book is typeset in League Gothic.

A CIP catalogue record for this book is available from the British
Library.

5 4 3 2 1

INTRODUCTION

Knock, knock! Who's there? Candice. Candice who? Candice jokes get any worse?

This, my chuckle buddies, is *Dave's Bad Jokes 2*. Can you believe it? They've let me give you more bad jokes, and now they're even worse!

After the incredible success of *Dave's Bad Jokes*, I checked my big giant document containing all the bad jokes you guys have ever sent me and it turns out there were even more in there than I could fit into a single book. Unless it was one of those NASA manuals for a spacecraft. They're massive! I did once read an actual book from NASA. It was about anti-gravity. I couldn't put it down! Boom! You see? Jokes galore.

Laughing is class. So is chuckling. And smiling. And even an eye-roll and a groan. They're all predictable reactions to the jokes in this book. Some of them are so funny they may even make some wee come out. But I checked with my lawyers and I'm not responsible for your pants, which is good news.

But I am responsible for thanking everyone who bought the last book and this book, listens to the jokes on the radio and, most important of all, submits bad jokes week in, week out. I am so grateful to you all.

Please send me pictures and videos of you enjoying this book. Please send me videos of oul' lads inflicting these jokes on their families. They're my favourites!

Here's to more jokes!

Love you guys,

Dave

I played Bonopoly last night. It's like Monopoly but the streets have no name.

A friend of mine got a job as a road cleaner who only works after dark. I don't know how he sweeps at night.

What do you call a caveman
wandering aimlessly?

A meanderthal.

I spotted Ronnie O'Sullivan at the garden centre yesterday.

I think he was eyeing up a plant.

I quit my part-time job as a treadmill tester.
I just felt like I wasn't going anywhere ...

If I had a euro for every time someone called me lazy, I'd have ... ah, forget it, I'll count it later.

I hate it when cashiers hold my money in the air to check if it's counterfeit. Listen, love, if I knew how to make fake money, I wouldn't be shopping in EuroGiant.

A man has been released from custody after being arrested for impersonating a helium balloon. A police spokesman said: 'We held him for a while, then let him go.'

Ever noticed that roofers tend to be really obnoxious? Maybe it's because they spend all their time looking down on people.

My kids are so open to experiencing food cultures. They'll try anything, from chicken nuggets and chips at an Indian restaurant to chicken nuggets and chips at a Mexican restaurant.

I told my granny not to throw her
false teeth at her Nissan Micra.
'You might denture car!'

I've just joined a new band called Cats' Eyes ... We mostly do middle-of-the-road stuff!

Which part of your body is the most reliable?

Well, you can always count on your fingers!

Bilbo was surprised to wake one morning and find that a Tesco had been built right next to his house. It was an unexpected item in the Baggins area.

What is Santa's favourite
heavy metal band?

Sleigh-er!

I've discovered the cheapest place to get kids' shoes is at the front of a bouncy castle.

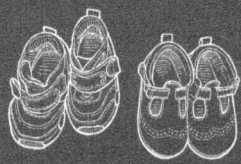

I'm going to try Velcro instead of shoelaces.
I mean, why knot?

For a period, Houdini used a trapdoor
in every single show he did.
I guess you could say it was a stage
he was going through.

My wife said I never listen.
At least, that's what I think she said.

A book hit me on the head the other day. I've only my shelf to blame.

My wife told me I was bad at snappy comebacks, but I said, 'No! You're bad at snappy comebacks!'

— •• • —

There's a new film about a tow bar
coming out next week. I just saw
the trailer for it today.

— • •• —

Two crisps are strolling down the road.

A guy passes in a car and asks,
'Do you guys want a lift?'

They reply, 'No thanks. We're Walkers.'

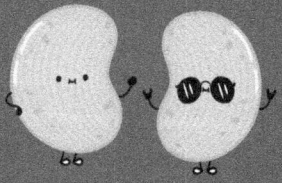

...

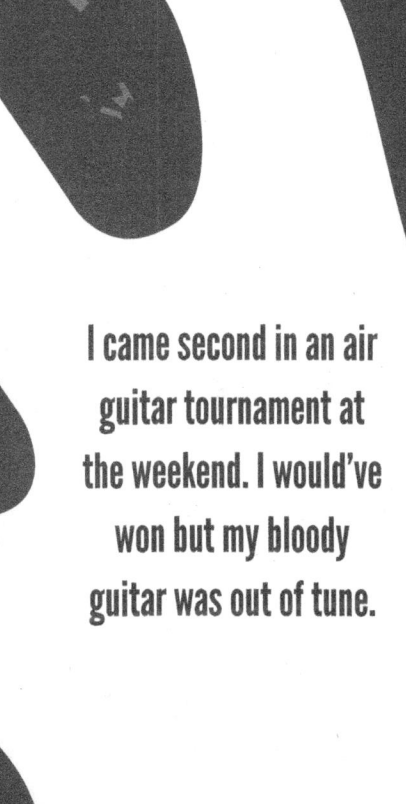

I came second in an air guitar tournament at the weekend. I would've won but my bloody guitar was out of tune.

The school phoned me today and said,
'Your son's been telling lies.'

I said, 'Well, he's very good at it
'cause I don't have any kids!'

What do you call a funny chef?

A gas cooker!

My friend got a job working in a mirror factory. I'm delighted for him. It's what he always saw himself doing.

My dad found out I had an
imaginary girlfriend. He said,
'You know, you could do better.'

'Thanks, Dad. That means a lot,' I replied.

'Er, I was talking to your girlfriend.'

Broken puppet for sale.
€5 or nearest offer.
No strings attached.

I tried to explain to my three-year-old daughter that it's perfectly normal to accidentally poop your pants but she's still making fun of me.

Eyelashes are supposed to stop things
going in your eyes but every time there's
something in my eye it's an eyelash.

Now, that's eyeronic!

I used to think innuendo
was an Italian suppository.

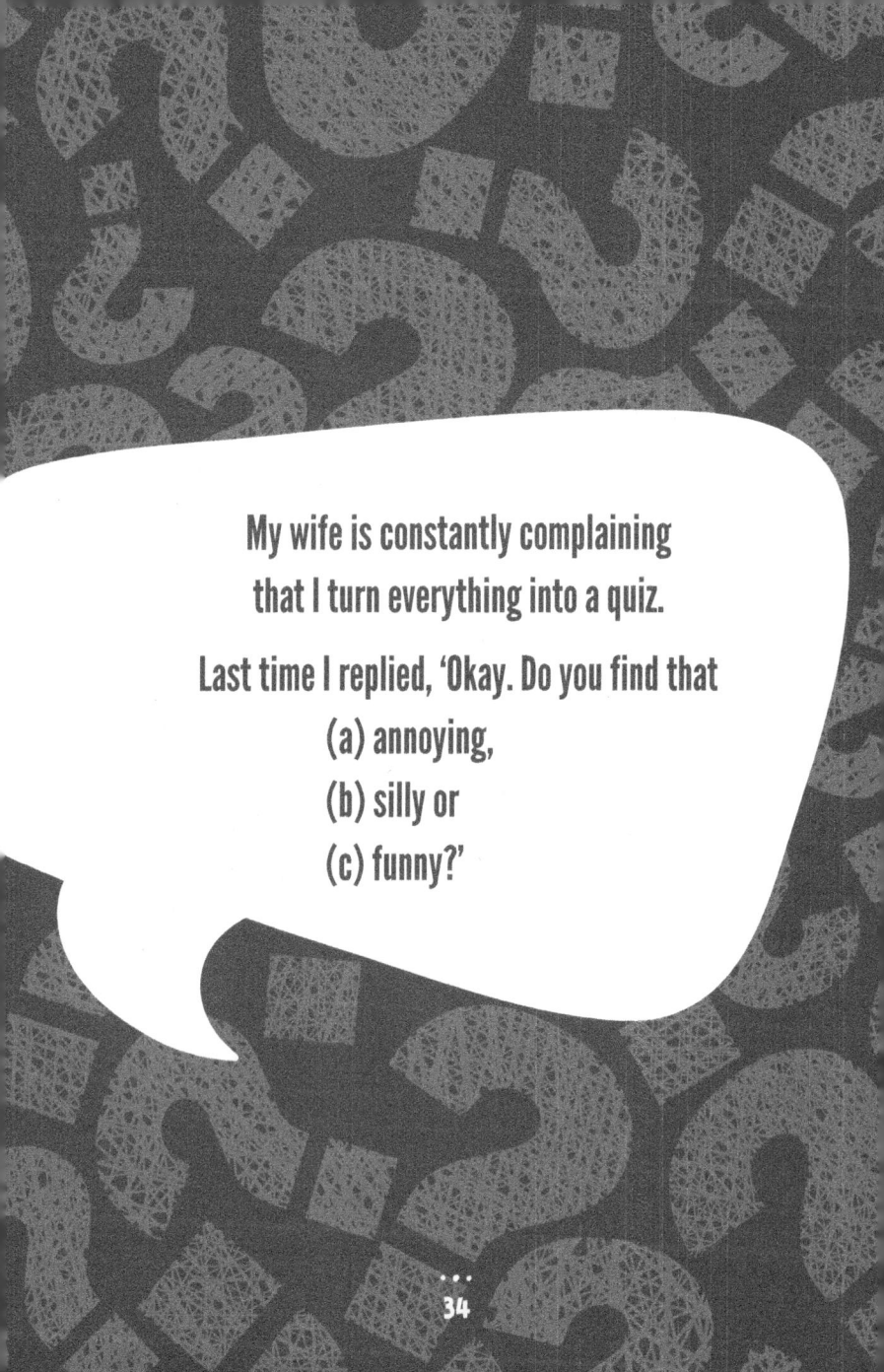

My wife is constantly complaining
that I turn everything into a quiz.

Last time I replied, 'Okay. Do you find that
(a) annoying,
(b) silly or
(c) funny?'

34

What do getting up at 4 a.m.
and a pig's tail have in common?

Twirly!

Where do American children
learn their ABCs?

In LMNtary school.

— •• • —

I try to eat healthily, but every
time I walk into a shop a chocolate
bar looks at me and snickers.

— • •• —

How many hipsters does it take to change a lightbulb?

Oh, it's a really obscure number. You've probably never heard of it.

. . .

What's the happiest furniture?

A table of contents.

I got a rejection letter from the University of Origami today. I'm not sure what to make of it.

I've worked really hard and got
quite good at ventriloquism.
Even if I do say so myself.

My wife has recommended I try lunges to stay in shape. That would be a big step forward for me.

What do pregnant cows and Monaghan have in common?

They're both near Caavvaan.

. . .

Why did the polar bear not get married?

Ah, the poor fella got cold feet!

After you die, which part of your body stops working last?

Your eyes – because they dilate.

On Valentine's Day last year, I told my girlfriend, 'I'm going to give you the sun, the moon and the stars.'

She was so excited until she unwrapped her new telescope, which I am currently using to find a new girlfriend.

What goes moo, baa, oink, woof, quack?

A cow that can speak five languages.

I started a fight with a mop.
To be fair, I wiped the floor with him!

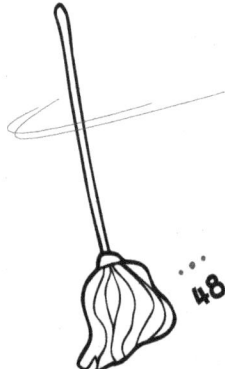

48

— • • • —

I sold my vacuum cleaner the other day. In fairness, all it was doing was collecting dust.

— • • • —

Just completed my new book, *The Most Essential Part of a Saxophone.* It's a good reed!

The Gardaí just rang me to say they
recovered my old sofa.
I thought that was nice of them –
it *was* starting to look a bit scruffy.

Why did the nurse go to art class?

So she could learn how to draw blood.

I went to an aquarium yesterday.
I was really disappointed. The main
attraction was supposed to be a great
white but it wasn't there any more.
Apparently it was a loan shark!

...

As soon as space travel is possible,
I'm moving from the Milky Way
galaxy to the Soymilky Way.
I'm galactose intolerant.

Who invented camping?

Henry the Tenth.

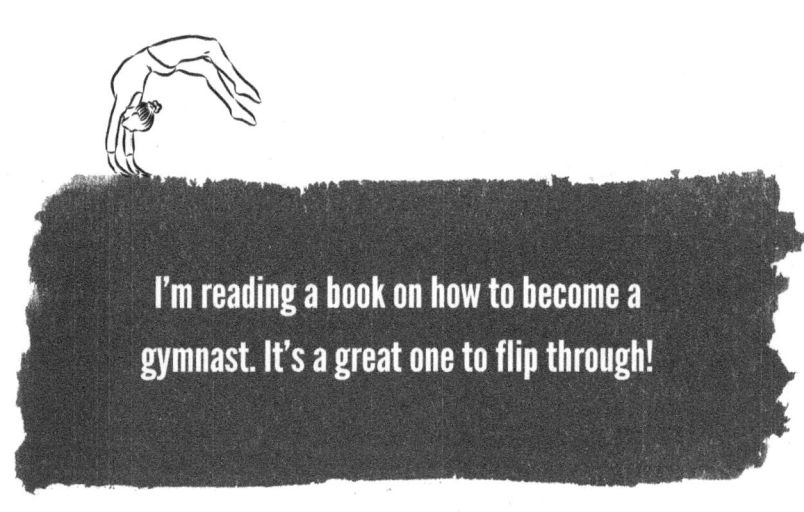

I'm reading a book on how to become a gymnast. It's a great one to flip through!

I've decided to set up a small business to buy old, unwanted jewellery. If you want a valuation, give me a ring.

— ・・・ —

I never thought selling keys would
pay off but I'll tell you what, it's
opened a few doors for me.

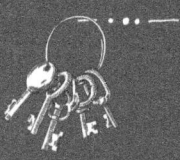

— ・・・ —

・・・

I asked my wife how to turn Alexa off.
She said, 'How about walking
through the room naked?'

My mam and dad always do things straightaway.
I call them my immediate family!

I've had enough of my local fishmongers selling undersized shellfish. I am going to take them to the small clams court.

— •• • —

I went to Tesco, but forgot my
Clubcard. Ugh. Pointless trip!

— • •• —

I gave my seat to an elderly lady on the bus today. I thought I was being polite, but now I've lost my job as a bus driver.

Ever thought of buying your own landfill site? Well, have I got some tips for you!

A mother says to her son, 'Right! Come on!
Get up! It's time for school!'

He says, 'Ah, Mam, I don't want to go! None of the kids
like me and the teachers are really mean to me.'

She says, 'For goodness' sake, Michael.
You're 46 years old and you're the headmaster.
You have to go!'

. . .

Beating a field of elite athletes and
winning the World Limbo Championship
was the low point of my career.

My imaginary friend's coming to stay
tonight so I've made up a bed for him!

Sadly, I've lost 20 per cent of my sight.

Sigh!

. . .

What's the best cheese to hide a horse in?

Mascarpone.

BREAKING NEWS ... There's an armed siege under way at the local zoo. The gunman has taken several ostriches!

Did you hear about the new corduroy pillows? They're making headlines everywhere!

Why can't you hear a pterodactyl go to the bathroom?

Because the 'p' is silent!

— ··· —

My daughter told me she's afraid
of the dark.

I told her, 'Wait till you start
paying for electricity and you'll be
scared of the light!'

— ··· —

I went to the funeral of the inventor of Optrex today. There wasn't a dry eye in the house.

My brother plays football for a team called
The Musketeers. They started the season well,
with three wins and a draw. All 4–1 and one 4–all!

I bumped into the inventor
of the globe last night.
It's a small world!

Went to a party last night thrown by the RNLI. Tell you what, they really know how to push the boat out!

I saw a guy running down the road with a cape on.

I shouted, 'Are you a superhero?'

He replied, 'No! I just haven't paid for my haircut!'

I tried to chat up the lady doing
X-rays at my local hospital but she
saw straight through me.

A large oil company is going to start
producing fuel from insect urine.
I think it's BP.

I threw a biscuit at my neighbour the other day but he ducked. Jammy dodger!

I witnessed a fight between an auctioneer and a hairdresser. They were going at it hammer and tongs!

One way or another, I'm gonna have
to stop quoting Blondie lyrics.

I'll tell you what makes me cross.
Lollipop ladies!

— • • • —

How warm are babies when they're born?
Womb temperature!

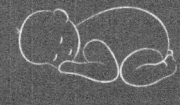

— • • • —

Just bought a cheap jack-in-the-box
that doesn't work properly.
No surprises there!

...

Writing groups in prisons:
they have their prose and cons!

My wife is insistent I shave the beard off. I keep telling her, 'I'm going nowhere near your face with a razor!'

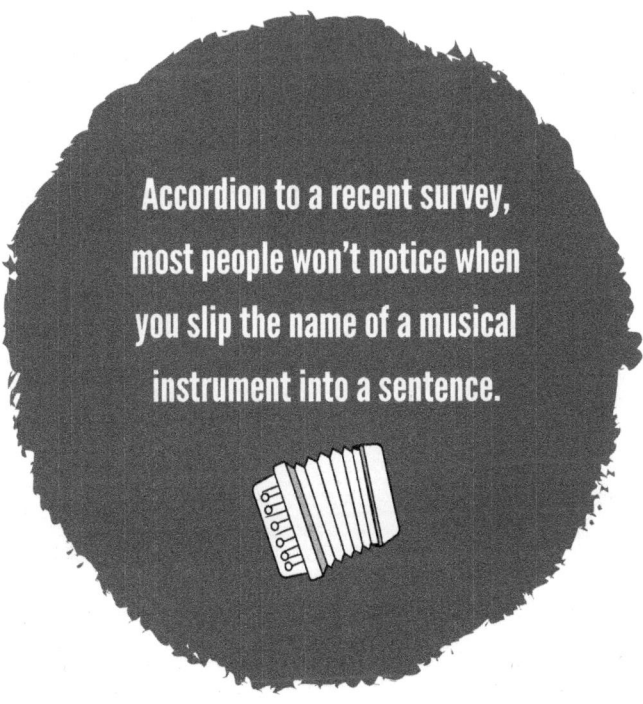

Accordion to a recent survey, most people won't notice when you slip the name of a musical instrument into a sentence.

My pet chicken likes to work out in the gym.
You should see the size of his pecks!

My mate lost his sense of touch.
You've got to feel for him.

91

The police are looking for me in connection with
the theft of thousands of inflatable airbeds.
I think I'd better lilo!

People criticise shops for selling Christmas stuff too early. Well, our supermarket has birthday cakes on the shelves already and mine isn't for another seven months!

My husband is threatening to leave me because of my obsession with wearing different clothes every half an hour. I said, 'Wait, I can change!'

I was sitting on the plane and this bloke tapped me on the shoulder and said, 'Excuse me. You're in my seat.'

I replied, 'But I've paid for a seat with a window at the front of the plane.'

He said, 'Well, you fly it then!'

Typical!

No one has turned up at Camouflage Club.

Again!

I went to a restaurant last night and the waiter said, 'For starters, there's badger soup, followed by roast badger and finishing with badger mousse.'

I asked, 'Is there anything else apart from badger?'

'No,' he replied. 'It's a sett menu!'

I've just been to my sister's house. She was counting out all the 1c and 2c coins from her handbag on the kitchen table. I thought to myself, 'She's going through the change!'

I'd love to get you into
Failed Escapologists' Club,
but sadly my hands are tied!

What do you call a pig with three eyes?

PIIIG!

I accidentally ordered the wrong packet of Hobnobs. I ordered Hotpoint but we have a Belling cooker.

Do you know which king
invented fractions?

Henry the 1/8th.

Ten years ago today, I asked my childhood sweetheart, my best friend and the most beautiful woman in the world to marry me.

All three said no.

What do you call having second thoughts about booking a hotel at the Native American casino?

Reservation reservation reservations!

Which month do soldiers like the least?

The month of March.

I got my wife a wind machine for her birthday. She was blown away!

Who wants to play Guess the Animal
Noise? Come on, it'll be a hoot!

Watching TV is a nightmare nowadays. Violence, fighting, cursing, swearing. And that's just getting the remote off the kids!

I've just heard on the news that
dentists are going on strike.
Brace yourselves!

The problem with political jokes is
that sometimes they get elected.

This may make me sound a bit big-headed,
but I can't get my jumper off.

I rang up my local swimming pool and asked, 'Is this the local swimming pool?'

He said, 'Well, it depends where you're calling from, I guess.'

I was sitting eating toast in my slippers
this morning when I thought to myself,
I really need to wash some plates.

My tailor was happy to fix my ripped shirt. Or sew it seams ...

I used to enjoy playing darts with my brother. But then he got too heavy to throw.

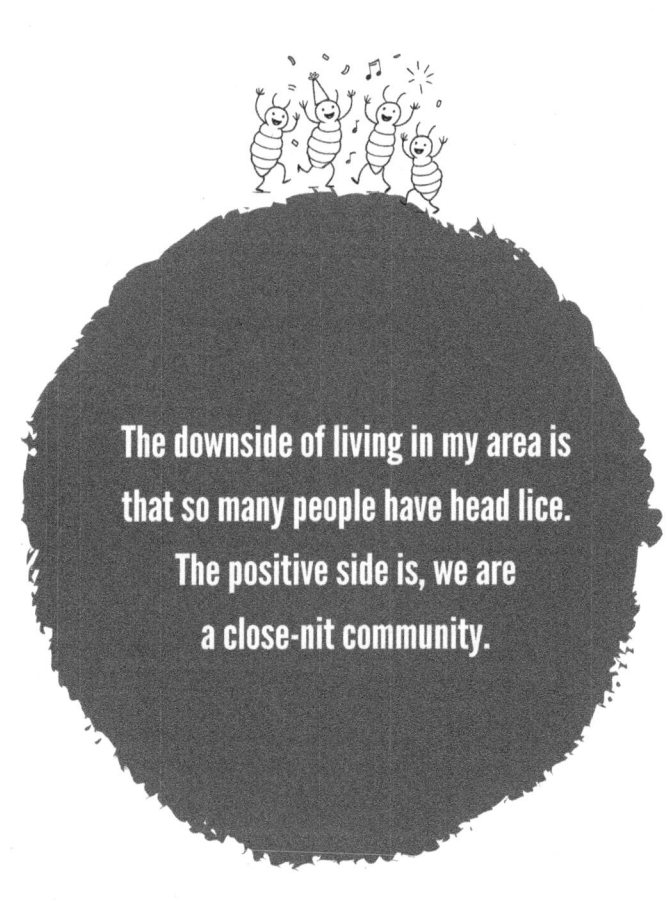

The downside of living in my area is that so many people have head lice. The positive side is, we are a close-nit community.

I was delivering leaflets yesterday on flatulence awareness. Unfortunately, I let one rip.

. . .

I'm able to hold a baby deer with either my right or left hand. I'm Bambidextrous!

If horses wear horseshoes,
what do camels wear?

Desert boots.

I took out a book about WD40 from
the local library earlier today.
It was in the non-friction section.

I've had enough of my wife's little games. I don't know why she has to buy the travel edition of everything.

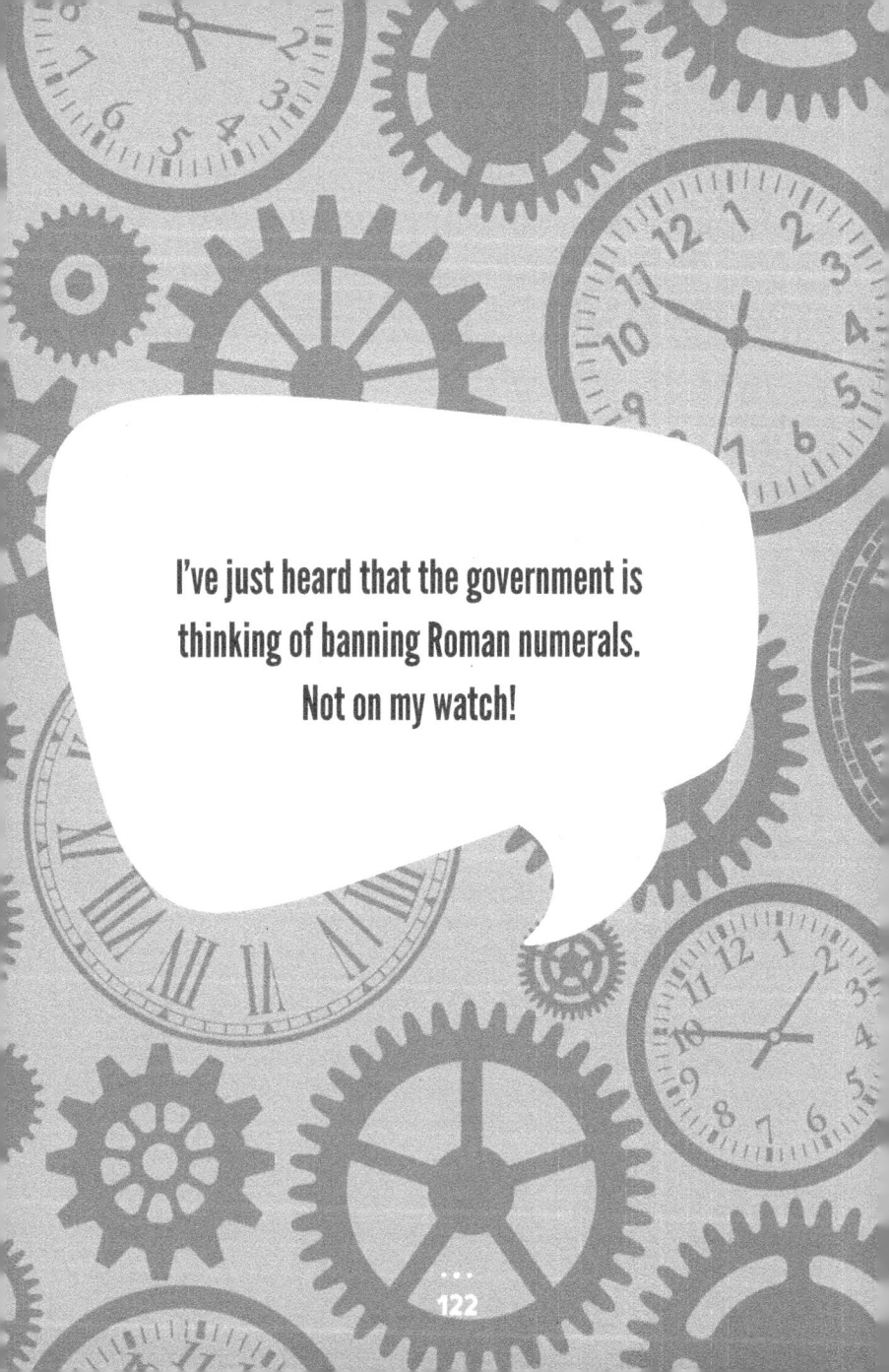

I've just heard that the government is thinking of banning Roman numerals.
Not on my watch!

I almost got into trouble earlier
when I accidently cut all the
leaves off the house plant. Luckily,
though, I managed to staple them
all back on. Phew! What a re-leaf!

My friend has designed an invisible plane.
I can't see it taking off.

What do you call a pile of cats?

A meowntain.

What do you call a wizard with a runny nose?

Harry Snotter.

You smell good.

Thanks. I use both nostrils!

What's faster than an escalator?

An esca-sooner.

I saw two lads on the street
arguing over a Leap Card.
It was a fare fight!

My wife told me, 'It's over,' and started to walk out on me. I just sat there. I love watching the end credits in the cinema!

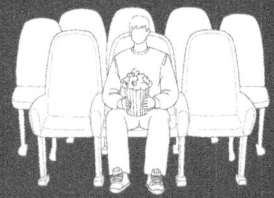

My dentist offered me helium gas.

I said, 'Helium gas? Will it stop the pain?'

He said, 'No, but it's very
funny when you scream.'

If a man says he'll fix something,
he'll fix it. There's no need to
remind him every six months.

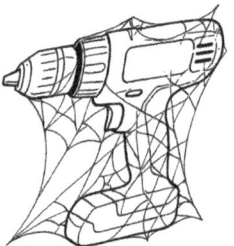

If a woman says she'll be ready in 15 minutes, she will be. There's no need to remind her every half hour.

What's got two arses and could kill you?

An assassin!

— ⋯ —

'How's the new diet going?'

'Ah, not good. I had six eggs for breakfast.'

'Six eggs? Scrambled?'

'No, Cadbury Creme.'

— ⋯ —

⋯

Where do wolves like to stay
on their holidays?

At the Howl-iday Inn!

It's really annoying when you go to someone's house and they ask you to take your shoes off. Like, 99 times out of 100, they don't even have a bouncy castle!

I put my earbuds under my pillow last night. When I woke up, they were gone and there was €5 instead! Argh! The bloody Bluetooth Fairy!

I bought coconut shampoo the other day, but when I got home I realised I don't even own a coconut.

My boss said, 'Dress for the job you
want, not for the job you have.'
So the next day I went in as Batman.

Ugh! I hate it when I get a splinter!
Hopefully I'll never get one again.
Touch wood!

Cadbury's have donated a giant chocolate
bar to the Central Bank of Ireland.
It's a massive Boost for the economy.

I accidentally deleted the manuscript of my new book, *100 Ways to Cure an Itch*. Looks like I'll have to start again from scratch.

My boyfriend wants me to blow air on him whenever he feels too warm. Honestly, I'm not a fan!

I was doing my driving test today.
The examiner asked me what
the most common road sign in
Ireland is. Apparently 'Wexford
Strawberries' is the wrong answer.

What do you call a woman who's
very good at playing darts?

Amy!

My neighbour claims his golden
retriever can bring a ball back
from half a mile away! I dunno.
That seems a bit far-fetched.

— .•. —

When your children are teenagers,
it's important to also have dogs so that
someone is happy when they see you.

— .•. —

People call me self-centred.
But that's enough about them!

I've just realised that I'm almost a millionaire. I have all the zeros, now I just need a one.

A huge shout-out to all those people who danced near the speakers back in the '80s! I said, A HUGE SHOUT-OUT TO ALL THOSE PEOPLE WHO DANCED NEAR THE SPEAKERS BACK IN THE '80S!

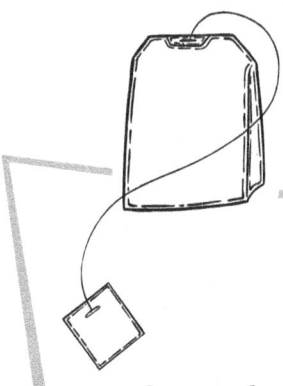

I was going to patent this new method
I invented for reusing tea bags,
but Barry's have taken out a
re-straining order against me!

It's like they always say: 'Walk a mile in someone else's shoes and you'll probably get an angry call from the manager at the bowling alley.'

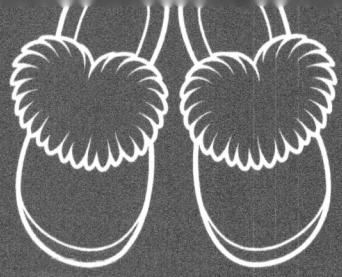

What's about a foot long and slippery?

A slipper!

I bought a bathroom scales from Amazon. It hasn't arrived yet. I think it's stuck out for delivery somewhere. I can't weight!

Went to the doctor yesterday with a suspicious-looking mole. He said they all look like that and I should have left him in my garden.

My mate Alan delivers beauty
products all over the country.
I call him Lorry Al.

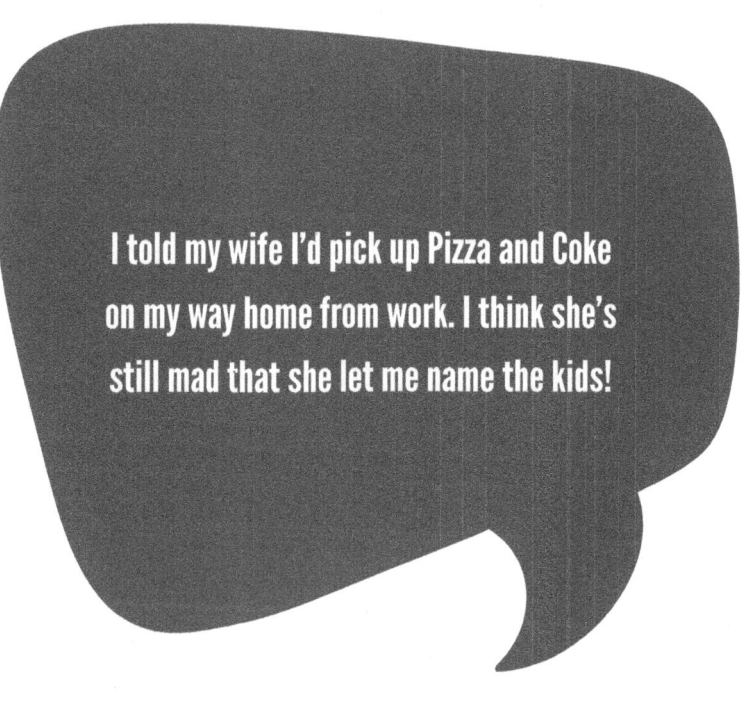

I told my wife I'd pick up Pizza and Coke on my way home from work. I think she's still mad that she let me name the kids!

Incontinence hotline. Please hold.

...

— ·· · —

I've a confession to make. I steal
chocolate bars from newsagents
using sleight of hand. I have quite
a few Twix up my sleeve!

— · ·· —

When I was a young boy the doctor told me I had a lazy eye. I'm sad to say that it has now spread to the rest of my body.

Zzzzz

I don't know how people have trouble sleeping.
I can do it with my eyes closed.

The best thing about having a husband is you can tell him any secret and he won't tell a soul, because, obviously, he wasn't listening in the first place.

I wanted to brighten up the garden,
so I planted some bulbs.

I've opened three birthday cards
today and I'm already €150 up.
God, I love being a postman!

What do you call two octopuses
that look the same?

Itentacle.

The other night I saw a couple
weaving all over the road. I mean,
honestly, get a loom!

I paused a film last night so I could make a cup of tea and now I've been fired by the cinema.

If you don't want to know the results of the staring contests, look away now!

Just got a job doing testing at the Rubik's Cube factory. It doesn't pay much but, hey, it's better than just sitting around twiddling my thumbs.

I just hired a professional worrier for €500 a month. I don't actually have €500 to spend every month but, sure, I'll let him worry about that!

I've joined the Exaggeration Club.
It's great! We meet up around
a million times a week.

I used to go out with a French lad
but he always stole my pancakes.
I think he was a crêpetomaniac.

— · · · · —

My favourite word is drool.
It just rolls off the tongue.

— · · · —

What kind of classes
do spiders attend?

Webinars!

When cooking kale, try adding some coconut oil.
It makes it a lot easier to scrape into the bin!

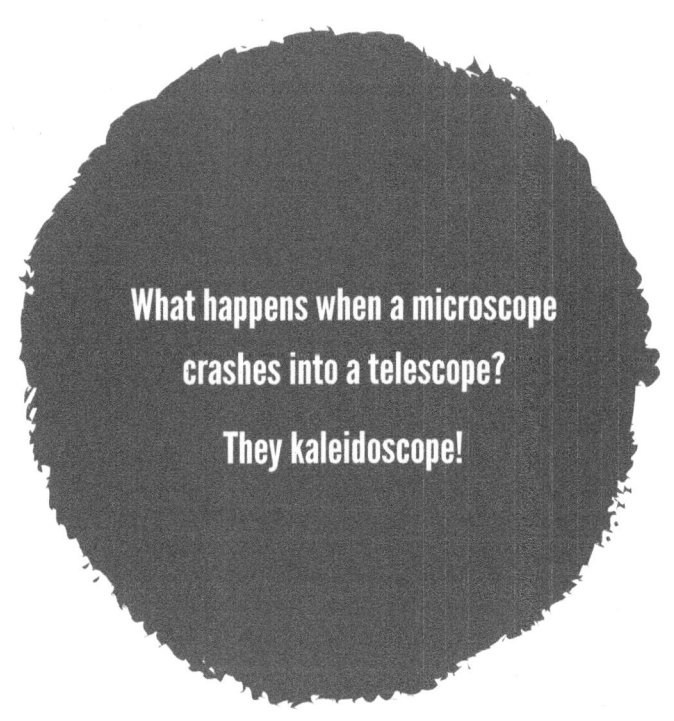

What happens when a microscope crashes into a telescope?

They kaleidoscope!

A man went into a shoe shop, picked a pair of shoes and asked for a size 12.

The shop assistant said, 'Sorry, sir. We don't have them in a 12.'

The man replied, 'Ah, grand. Then I'll take two pairs of size 6s.'

Once again, I've entered our town's annual Tightest Hat Competition. This year I'm really hoping I can pull it off.

...

I just stepped on a cornflake.
Does that make me a cereal killer?

I'm finally dealing with my
procrastination issues.
Just you wait and see!
Any day now!

I did badly in school, I mean REALLY badly.
I even failed the easiest subject to pass,
Religion! I mean, Jason Cripes!
How can you fail Religion?

My wife said, 'You're so unromantic.
I bet you don't even know what my
favourite flower is.'

'Is it Odlum's?' I asked.

Went to PC World today.
Blimey! You've got to watch
what you say in there.

My wife and I took the kids to the zoo last week. Next weekend we're heading back to see if they have settled in.

There I was, having a great time
with my four-year-old on the
swings at the park, until he told
me he was sick of pushing me and
it was time to go home.

— • •• —

What does a ghost
panda bear eat?

Bam-BOO!

...

Oh, look at me! I'm so posh and fancy,
I had frogs' legs for dinner!
Well, I bit the bottom half off a Freddo.

Oh, yeah! When Miley Cyrus dances naked and licks a hammer, it's 'art'. When I do it, I've had one too many and get kicked out of Woodies.

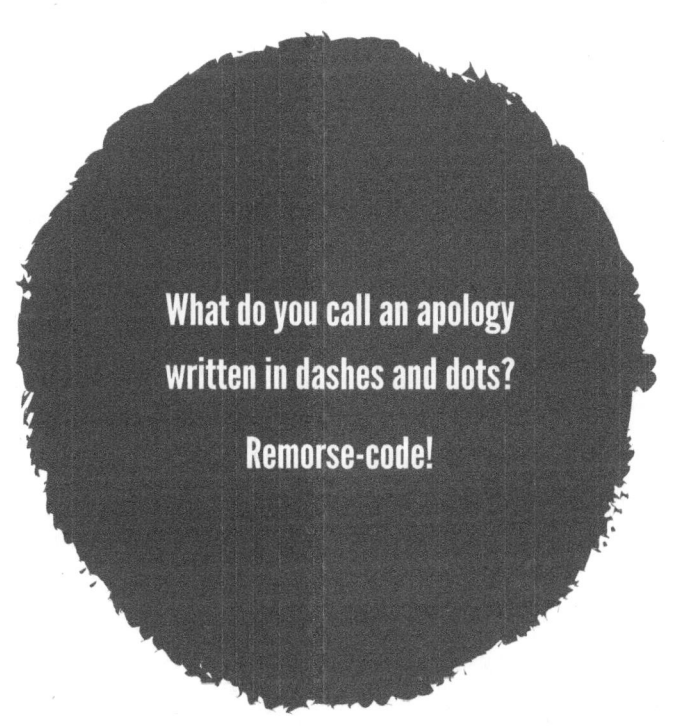

What do you call an apology
written in dashes and dots?

Remorse-code!

The hardest part about making
skimmed milk is definitely
throwing the cow across the lake.

I asked the missus where she
wanted to go on holiday this year.

She said, 'What about the Canaries?'

I said, 'Ah, sure, the neighbours
will look after them.'

I just had a bloke knock at my door.
When I answered he said, 'Hi. I've had
a call to come and tune your guitar.'

I said, 'But I never called you.'

He said, 'I know – your neighbours did.'

I've been trying to get hold of
my judo instructor for ages but
he's a hard man to pin down.

I hired a kid to paint my porch.
When he came back to get paid,
he said, 'By the way, missus.
That was a BMW, not a Porsche!'

I read an inspirational quote the other day that said, 'Do what you love and the money will follow.' I ate a whole pizza, took a nap, and watched TV. Now we wait!

I always laugh when I see one
of those tiny Mexican dogs!
Chihauhuahahahahaha!

I keep telling my wife that she should
wear appropriate gardening attire.
But she's digging in her heels.

— •• • —

What do you call an Irish hand
drum made out of dog skin?

A Bow-wow-rán!

— • •• —

• • •

My new dog keeps barking at common people. Turns out I've bought a Jarvis Cocker spaniel.

When is the best time to start
using your trampoline again?

Spring!

I just posted a photo of myself at the gym, and it was flagged and removed as 'fake news'.

'I'd like to make a reservation for a table for two, please.'

'Sir, you do know that this is McDonald's?'

'Oh, sorry. I'd like to make a McReservation for a table for two, please.'

I'm thinking of starting my own business recycling discarded chewing gum. I just need a bit of help getting it off the ground.

What do you call it when one
banana eats another?

Cannibananabalism!

It's a lovely crisp morning.

I've eaten three bags already.

I bought a book today called *Overcoming Kleptomania*. Well, I say bought ...

Banks should do a better job of keeping their ATMs filled. This is the fifth one I've been to that says insufficient funds.

— • • • —

I met a bulb today. He was lovely.
I asked if he was working over the
Christmas and he said,
'Ah, yeah. On and off.'

— • • • —

• • •

My wife says she wants a cat for Christmas. Normally I do a turkey but, hey, if it'll make her happy ...

I don't always listen to heavy metal,
but when I do, so do the neighbours.

I'm still really angry at my classmates for voting me 'Most Likely to Hold a Grudge'!

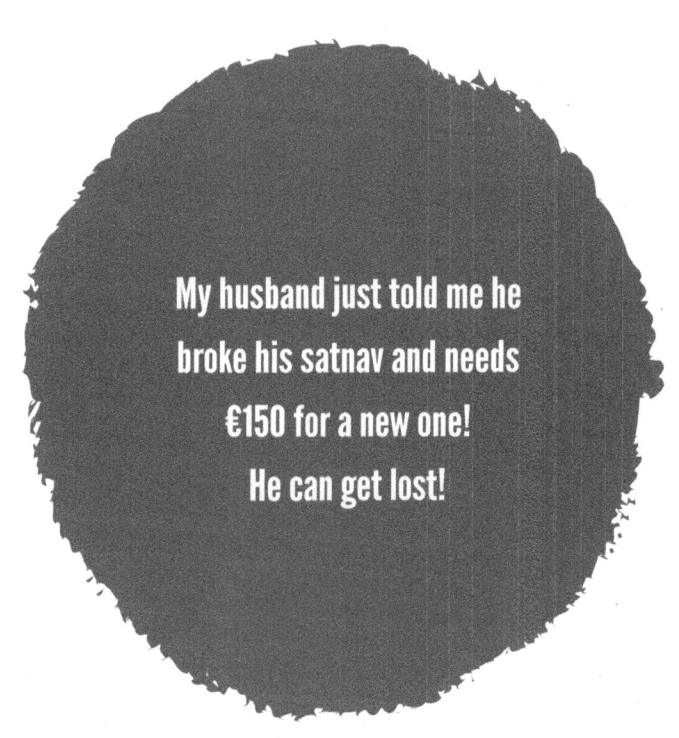

My husband just told me he
broke his satnav and needs
€150 for a new one!
He can get lost!

I bought a brand new €800 leather jacket online for only €20! When I examined it, the only fault was the left arm was half an inch shorter than the other two.

I thought I'd be trendy and try one of these 'alternative milks'. I don't know what a magnesia is, but it made my cornflakes taste horrible!

Some people have been saying I'm going through a midlife crisis, but I can't hear them over the sound of my awesome new motorbike.

...

Why are giraffes so slow
to apologise?

Because it takes them so
long to swallow their pride.

My parents raised me as an only child,
which really annoyed my sisters.

I messed up big time. I tried
to walk like an Egyptian.
Now I need to see a Cairopractor.

Both of my marriages have been very disappointing.
My first husband left me, the second one didn't.

Yesterday the Gardaí arrested me for unsolicited spooning. I wasn't charged, they just held me over-night. Which I loved, by the way.

My doctor has finally found a way
to stop me glowing in the dark.
I'm delighted!

A Trojan horse walks into a bar. He walks up to the barman and says, '362 pints, please.'

I was in my local café and my phone kept receiving pictures of stews and casseroles. I couldn't work it out. Then I copped on! Sure I was connected to a wireless hotpot!

Finally! My bills are washed,
my laundry is paid, the clothes are
baking and dinner is in the dryer.
I've got this!

I just read a book called
*How to Clear Leaves from
Your Driveway* by Ray King.

What kind of trousers
does a psychic wear?

Just a paranormal pants!

I resent being called a hoarder.
The reason I keep these old cables in a
drawer is just in case somebody ever wants
to connect a Nokia N95 to a fax machine.

My neighbour told me my homemade wine was rubbish but I think that's just sour grapes.

My doctor told me to eat more greens.
Fair enough, but it's a right pain
sorting through those wine gums.

I went trampolining on
Saturday, Sunday and Monday.
That's three days on the bounce.

I always set two wake-up alarms:
one for the person I want to be,
and one for the person I am.

If anyone has any ideas on how
to correct cosmetic surgery that
went horribly wrong, I'm all ears!

What's a tumble dryer's
favourite chocolate?

Lindt!

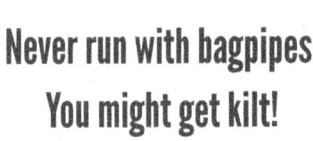

Never run with bagpipes.
You might get kilt!

I just renewed my car insurance and, as we were wrapping up, the lady asked me, 'Before you go, sir, do you have any pets?'

'Yes, I have a dog,' I replied.

'Oh, great! Would you also like to insure your dog with us?'

'Nah, it's okay. He can't drive.'

I wanted a dog but my dad said
they're too loud. So I got a pet tree.
It's a lot like having a pet dog,
but the bark is much quieter!

A man walks into a library and asks, 'Excuse me. Do you have any books on how to improve poor eyesight?'

'No, we don't,' says the barman.

Just a quick shoutout to all the footpaths out there. Thanks for keeping me off the streets!

I tried to take a picture of a wheat field but it turned out all grainy.

• • •

I took my wife out for a romantic meal for our anniversary last night. She kept saying she wanted to pay for the meal. I said, 'We've nearly lost them! Keep running!'

'Doctor! Doctor! I've developed
a terrible phobia of trains.'

'Are you taking anything for it?'

'Yeah. The bus.'

I'm just off to the gym. I'm not telling you this to brag but just so you know where to send the ambulance later.

Which crisps can never get to the point?

Waffles.

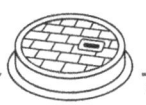

I've been fired from my job cleaning the sewers.
Well, that's twenty years down the drain.

• • •

My boss called the whole company in during lunch yesterday and announced that there was a thief in the office kitchen. I was so shocked I nearly spat out his sandwich!

I figured out how to avoid getting parking tickets.
I've snapped off both my windscreen wipers.

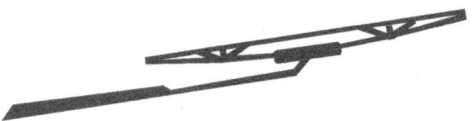

Two lads are driving up the road.
They come to a junction.

The fella driving asks,
'What's it like on your side?'

The other lad says, 'Similar to yours,
just no steering wheel or pedals.'

— • • • —

What do you call a woman
with two toilets in her house?

Lulu.

— • • • —

Why do Italian policemen always carry bread around with them?

Focaccia'n criminals!

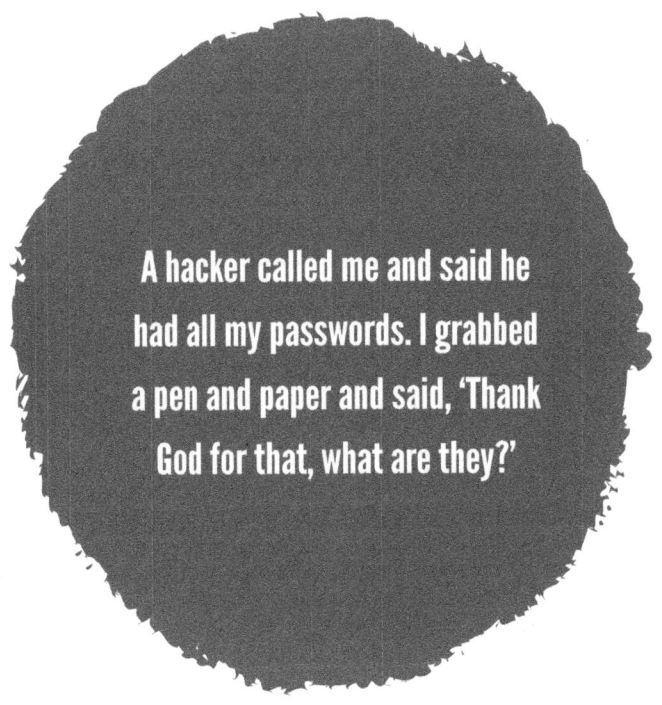

A hacker called me and said he had all my passwords. I grabbed a pen and paper and said, 'Thank God for that, what are they?'

I woke up from a deep sleep in a panic thinking I was late for work. Thankfully, I was already at work.

I went to the shop earlier and said, 'Excuse me, can I pay by card?'

The lady at the till said, 'Yeah, no problem. What card do you have?'

I said, 'The six of spades.'

I've decided on my new career.
I'm going to be a backwards stripper.
I come out on stage naked, and people
pay me to put my clothes back on.

When I was a kid, bedtime was 9 p.m. And I couldn't wait to be a grown-up so I could go to bed anytime I wanted. Turns out that is also 9 p.m.